TRACING ROOTS

African American Genealogy Unearthed
Step-by-Step Guide

Jeannette Golden

Table of Contents

Tracing Roots Introduction

My journey into genealogy research was never something that I had an interest in doing or something that I sought out to do. It was a passing curiosity that developed into a "thing" that has become a part of my life. I can't say I saw "it" coming or understood what "it" was. But "it" has been a quest that I am thankful for.

I am forever indebted to my family for their willingness to share and participate in this journey of discovery. To my aunts and uncles who allowed me to randomly call whenever I had a question and pick their brains, Thank You! To the Kings of our family who guarded and protected the Queens of our family, Thank You.

In this document I will take you through my learning process and the resources that I used and the connections that were made. My research is from an African American perspective, and I will share my thoughts and challenges thought out. A specific outline is provided for African American Genealogy Research.

Follow the steps outlined in this book and you will have a solid basis to begin your research. No formal education is required. All you need is a strong desire to learn more about yourself and your ancestors.

Common Genealogy Terms

Genealogy

- a line of descent traced continuously from an ancestor.

- a record or account of the ancestry and descent of a person, family, group, etc.

- the study of family ancestries and histories.

Ancestor

- a person, typically one more remote than a grandparent, from whom one is descended.

Maternal

- relative related through the mother's side of the family.

Paternal

- relatives related through the father's side of the family.

Generations

- all people born and living at about the same time frame.

Chattel

- one person has total ownership of another.

Grandma's Life Lessons

I would like to offer ten valuable lessons or basic ground rules that were shared with me by my grandmother. Remember them as you begin your research. They will come in handy and have been constant reminders in this journey.

1. Children are not responsible for the circumstances or the families that they were born into.

2. Family history is not "gossip".

3. Be patient and learn to listen.

4. Don't assume anything. When in doubt, ask. Don't make an ass of yourself by guessing.

5. You don't know, what you don't know.

6. Facts are facts!

7. Family is everything and some families are not like ours.

8. **Be proud of who you are.**

9. If you don't know your history (roots) or where you're from, you can easily fall for anything.

10. Your past does not define your future.

Step 1 – Interviewing Family

Interview Family Members: *Start with what you know. Talk to relatives, especially the older generations, to gather names, dates, and places.*

This is the very foundation of your research. When you are starting out, you should assume you know nothing but are actively waiting for someone to paint a picture of who "they are". If you're lucky, they will connect you to how you are related.

Be patient, and don't try to tell the interviewee what you think you know. Some people may resist being interviewed and may not want to talk to you. It's easier to ask for their help as you want to discover more about your family and who you are. It's okay if they don't want to talk the first time. You'll have many opportunities to ask again.

I was fortunate that my grandmother, the matriarch of our family, shared our family history with me. It was truly amazing. She knew facts and stories. She knew each of her grandparents, uncles, and aunts. She knew their children and where they lived.

She made references to places as if "I should know". She was right, I should have known so that I could pass that history on to the next generation.

I took copious notes and tried my best to keep up. But, in this instance I realized that she had waited generations to share her knowledge and it was my role to document what she was telling me. It was truly life changing as I learned about our ancestors.

Grandma shared stories of how our family came to live in this little town of Batesville, Mississippi. It was profoundly clear to me that she was the keeper of our family history. And now, it was passed on to me. In that moment, all I could think was I had to get it right. I had to write it down and capture the significance of this moment.

My Mom was there with me, and you could see that something generational was happening. My Mom was proud that I was there to hear our family history and legacy spoken to her daughter, from her mother! I was happy that my mother was present as I knew this conversation was way over my head and there were bound to be questions.

My grandmother spoke for hours, and I wrote down as best that I could. The names were not familiar, the places were unknown. Freemen, Irby, up the creek, up by Cousin Lula's house, Grand Paw Rufus. Lord, what have I gotten myself into?

My grandmother made no formal request that I document what she told me. It was implied that I better give her something to make sure I had properly documented what she told me. No pressure!

Lesson: #3

Be patient and learn to listen.

Step 1 – Summary Interviewing Family

Interviewing Family Members:

- Gather oral histories and personal stories from family members and neighbors that may not be documented elsewhere.

- Record interviews and take notes on family lore and anecdotes.

The Value of the Older Generation:

- Engage with older relatives to learn about family history and obtain original documents.

- Respect and preserve their stories and materials for future generations.

Community Histories:

- Research the history of the communities where your ancestors lived to understand non-traditional family structures.

Step 2 – Building a Family Tree

Build a Family Tree: *Use online platforms or software to organize the information you collect.*

When I began my research, I was not aware of any online resources. I'm sure they existed. But I had no idea of what I was doing except recording what my grandmother shared with me.

The spoken word! Our family history was not something that was formally written. It had been shared by spoken word from the matriarchs of our family. Those stories passed through generations.

Our family history centers around stories of Big Lou. My grandmother shared that Big Lou was a slave and came to Batesville, Mississippi from Nottoway County, Virginia. She was believed to be the mother of 21 children. Those children were separated between slave owners and moved to Memphis, Tennessee, and some parts of Louisiana, near New Orleans. They had different surnames (last names) and could potentially be anywhere in the United States. The surnames that my grandmother mentioned were, Irby, Perry, Black and Steward.

I did not understand the significance of these surnames until later during my research. I, as an African American researcher, now understand that much of our history has been passed through generations by the Spoken Word. It was now my responsibility to document that which had been spoken to me!

Fact, the same story of Big Lou was spoken to her children who were taken from her, and relocated throughout the country, so they would understand their history of slavery, separation, and resilience. More important, they would know and value their roots, heritage and that they too would speak this history to their children.

That spoken word has been passed down through generations and among siblings. These words have reached those siblings who were separated from their mother and community decades ago. That legacy cannot be erased or altered.

Lesson: #9

If you don't know your history (roots) or

where you're from,

you can easily fall for anything.

Step 2 – Summary Building a Family Tree

Building a Family Tree from Scratch:

- Start with yourself and work backward. List your parents, grandparents, sibling, and children. Record as much information that you have available about **you**.

- Document each generation with sources and citations.

- A citation is a note describing your source of information and recording exactly where you found it.

The National Archives is a valuable source of information and is an important asset as you begin your research. It includes many forms that can be downloaded from the computer and printed. Some of the sources included:

Family Group Forms
- <u>Ancestral Chart</u>
- <u>Family Group Sheet</u>
- <u>Modern Genealogy Tree</u>
- <u>Traditional Tree</u>

Family Group Sheet

Here is a snapshot of the Family Group Sheet that I suggest you use to begin building your family tree. It is available from the National Archives.

Family Group Sheet

Husband			Occupation(s)	
	Date	Place	Immigration	
Born			Naturalization	
Christened			Military Service	
Died			Cause of Death	
Buried			Date of Will	
Married				
Father			Other Marriages	
Mother				

Wife (maiden name)			Occupation(s)	
	Date	Place	Immigration	
Born			Naturalization	
Christened			Military Service	
Died			Cause of Death	
Buried			Date of Will	
Father			Other Marriages	
Mother				

Other Information/Records (ie. Census, Passports, etc…)

National Archives and Records Administration   NARA's website is www.archives.gov   NA Form 14135 (2/13)

Source(s)

1. National Archives

Step 3 – Getting Organized

Keep records organized: *Gather your research and organize what you've learned and begin the process of writing down facts.*

Having received so much valuable information can be overwhelming. What do you do with it? How is it going to make sense? The simplest method is to use the Family Data Sheets that you created in Step Two and follow the guidelines listed under Tracing Roots Genealogy Guide.

The key to this step is to be prepared to organize your thoughts and findings. It is extremely important to document the sources of this information. Build your own master copy as a starting point for your research.

A master copy is a collection of information and sources that you've compiled. Some information will have a higher degree of certainty about its authenticity and correctness. A good example is the Family Group Sheet that you developed for yourself.

Other information compiled will require additional research and verification.

Lesson: #5

You don't know, what you don't know.

Step 4 - Reviewing Home Documents

Review Home Documents: *Look for old photographs, documents, letters, and other artifacts that might provide clues.*

If you have heard the phrase, "A picture is worth a thousand words", looking at old photos will help bring the past forward. Photos provide details of how someone lived their lives. They can provide details of what was happening, where they lived or traveled. More important, it connects a name with a face. That humanizes our ancestors and connects us to our past.

Old letters are treasures especially when they are written to or from someone you love. I have letters that were written to me by my grandmother, my great auntie and by my mother. Personally, those letters let me know that someone wanted to connect with me. They took the time to send me a note of love. I'm not certain that an email will have the same effect.

One of the treasures that my grandmother provided were old obituaries from people she considered family or friends. Honestly, I was not warm to these documents, and I resisted for probably the first few years in my research. Something about an obituary saddened me.

But my grandmother kept them for years, so I knew there was a purpose. I trusted my grandmothers' wisdom. So, despite all my mixed emotions I proceeded.

I began to read the papers, and the stories jumped from the pages. This document was not about a person who died. It was, in fact, a short biography of the life the person lived, their family, friends, and their impact on those who would read this document. Each document is literally a family tree. When you read them with understanding you will see that someone took the time to paint a picture of how this person lived.

Lesson: #2

Family history is not "gossip".

Step 5 − Using Your Master Data

Research Your Master Data: *Validate or fill in gaps in your master data.*

You should feel confident in your master data. I have listed some of the resources that I use in my research. It is important that you understand the purpose for your research. Some facts will alarm you and some facts may hurt you. Be prepared to endure this emotional roller coaster.

Understanding black history and its roots in slavery has been the most painful part of my research. But they are facts that you must understand as it is crucial to really knowing and understanding who you are.

I know about the journey our ancestors took, their arrival in Batesville, Mississippi and their departure from Nottaway County, Virginia. Seen as property and uprooted from their communities and families.

I know the name of the slave owner who purchased slaves to work on *his* plantation. My ancestors purchased as chattel (a personal possession). I know the records that he kept of the chattel that he owned. My ancestors that he did not have the decency to give a proper name. Boy, Gal with a simple count of **his** chattel! Their true identities never written or captured in historical records or slave manifest. Simply, they arrived on this ship and became chattel. Those facts anger me.

I know the name and face of a slave who was repeatedly raped at the hands of her "master". Who after giving birth to his child, he later raped and impregnated his own daughter. A slave owner who later separated *his* children from their mother and sold them to *his* brothers and scattered them across the south.

It is true that you may never know the real names of your ancestors who arrived on vessels from whatever foreign country. But I promise that when you review those slave records and manifest, you will feel the resilience and survival! I've picked people from these manifest and I have claimed them as my ancestors. Therefore, their suffering, endurance, survival, and LIVING, were not in vain. I choose to celebrate them as my family.

Remember these, Lessons!

Lesson: #1

Children are not responsible for the circumstances or the families that they were born into.

Lesson: #6

Facts are facts!

Lesson: #7

Family is everything and some families are not like ours.

Lesson: #10

Your past does not define your future.

Genealogy Resources

Here's a short list of genealogy resources to assist in your research:

1. Online Resources:

- Begin with popular genealogy online websites like Ancestry.com, FamilySearch.org, and MyHeritage.com. Other online resources exist.

- Use online databases and digital archives to find records and documents.

2. United States Archives:

- Explore the National Archives (archives.gov) for federal records, military records, and immigration data.

- Check state, city, and county archives for region-specific information.

3. Soundex:

- Use the Soundex system to locate records that have similar sounding names which may have varied spellings. Remember that many people of color were forbidden to have the ability to read or write. Even if they could, that fact was not openly shared.

4. Census Data:

- Census records can provide household information, occupations, and more. It is not uncommon to find children listed in multiple households. Depending on when the data was collected, you may find children visiting or living with grandparents or other family members.

- Access U.S. Federal Census data every ten years from 1790 to 1950. The availability of the 1950's Census is an opportunity to speak with relative who are still living.

Remember, genealogy research is like detective work; it requires patience, diligence, and attention to detail. Remain persistent and unwavering.

Tracing Roots Step-by-Step Guide

Here's a guide to help you get started with genealogy research for African Americans:

Getting Started:

1. **Interview Family Members**: Start with what you know. Talk to relatives, especially the older generations, to gather names, dates, and places.

2. **Build a Family Tree**: Use online platforms or software to organize the information you collect.

3. **Keep records organized**: Gather your research and organize what you've learned and begin the process of writing it down.

4. **Review Home Documents**: Look for old photographs, documents, letters, and other artifacts that might provide clues.

5. **Research Your Data**: Validate or fill in gaps in your master data.

Identifying African Lineage:

- **DNA Testing**: Consider using DNA testing services to help identify genetic links to specific regions in Africa.

- **Historical Context**: Understand the history of the slave trade and its routes to determine possible areas of origin[22].

Using Slave Records and Manifests:

- **Slave Databases**: Explore databases like the Trans-Atlantic Slave Trade Database to find information on voyages and enslaved individuals[6].

- **National Archives**: Check for slave manifests and other related records in the National Archives Catalog[16].

Understanding the Great Migration:

- **Census Records**: Use census data to track movements, especially post-1910 when the Great Migration began[24].

- **City Directories**: Look for ancestors in city directories of northern cities where many African Americans relocated.

Researching Non-Traditional Family Homes:

- **Community Histories**: Research the history of the communities where your ancestors lived to understand non-traditional family structures.

- **Oral Histories**: Collect stories from family members and neighbors that may not be documented elsewhere.

Exploring the History of Slavery:

- **Slavery Era Records**: Investigate records from the slavery era, such as plantation records, wills, and estate inventories for clues about ancestors[6].

- **Freedmen's Bureau Records**: Post-Civil War records from the Freedmen's Bureau can be invaluable for tracing ancestors during the Reconstruction era.

Avoiding Surname Common Pitfalls:

- **Assuming Names Stayed the Same**: Be aware that surnames may have changed, especially after emancipation[11].

- **Overlooking Segregated Records**: Search for records that may have been segregated, such as "Colored" sections in directories or cemeteries.

- **Not Considering Alternate Spellings**: Be flexible with name spellings, as they were often recorded phonetically. This is extremely common in communities of color.

Remember, genealogy research is a journey that will take time. Be patient, stay organized, be prayed up and keep an open mind as you uncover your African American family's history. Keep this step-by-step guide handy and refer to it often.

Source(s)

1. Tracing African Ancestry using DNA | by Andre Kearns | Medium

2. 10 Databases for Researching Enslaved Ancestors - ThoughtCo

3. Slave Manifests - National Archives Catalog • FamilySearch

4. Great Migration | Definition, History, & Facts | Britannica

5. African American genealogy - Wikipedia

6. African American Genealogy: A Guide to Finding Your Ancestors Online

7. African American Genealogy - Enoch Pratt Free Library

8. 4 Easy-to-Follow Steps for African American Genealogy Newbies

9. Find your African American ancestors • FamilySearch

10. African American Genealogy • FamilySearch

11. Quick Guide to African American Records • FamilySearch

12. Researching Formerly Enslaved African Americans - FamilySearch

13. Avoiding Common Pitfalls in Family History Research

14. How the Smithsonian can help research African American family history

15. Your African American Genealogy Research Guide - Family Tree Magazine

16. African American Genealogy Challenges: What You Need to Know - FamilySearch

17. AAHGS | HOME PAGE

18. New genealogy method helps fill gaps in African American ancestry ...

19. How to Uncover Slave Genealogy | A Guided Journey

20. The Effects of Slavery and Emancipation on African American Families ...

21. The Relationship Between African Americans and Africa - AAIHS

22. Partners in time: Reconnecting African Americans with their tribes of ...

23. Tracing African Ancestry using DNA | by Andre Kearns | Medium

24. A Cheat Sheet for Researching African American Ancestors - The Root

25. Great Migration: Definition, Causes & Impact | HISTORY

26. Great Migration (African American) - Wikipedia

27. The Great Migration (1910-1970) | National Archives

28. Microsoft Co-pilot

Moving Past Obstacles

Breaking through genealogical brick walls can be challenging, but here are some strategies that might help you move past these obstacles:

1. Reevaluate Your Research:

- Take a step back and review your existing research for potential errors or assumptions that need rechecking. *Lesson #6: Facts are facts.*

2. Broaden Your Search:

- Look beyond direct ancestors and research siblings, cousins, and other relatives who might lead you to new information. Consider alternate family structures.

3. Utilize Different Record Types:

- Explore a variety of records such as yearbooks, church records, land deeds, wills, probate records, and court documents that may provide new clues. Visit the local county office as many records may not be available online.

4. Look for Alternate Spellings:

- Names may have been spelled differently in historical records, so consider various phonetic spellings and transcriptions.

5. Research the Local Community:

- Investigate Friends and Neighbors of your ancestors for indirect evidence that can break down walls.

6. Use DNA Testing:

- Genetic genealogy can uncover relationships and ancestors not found in traditional records. This area is building interest as the results provide more relevant information. Still, many are concerned about privacy issues and are reluctant to use DNA testing. However, DNA testing provided my first valuable link to my paternal family.

7. Seek Out Local Histories:

- Local histories can provide context and clues about the lives of your ancestors and their communities. Check local libraries, church records and newspapers.

8. Collaborate with Other Family Researchers:

- You will be amazed that there are many other distant cousins and family members who are researching just like you. Connect with them first.

- Join genealogy forums, social media groups, or societies to share information and get new perspectives.

9. Hire a Professional:

- If you're still stuck, consider hiring a professional genealogist who may have access to more resources or different strategies. This is not something that I tried. Introducing someone to your research, who has no vested interest in your research, never appealed to me.

Remember, persistence is key in genealogy. Each brick wall is an opportunity to learn more about the research process and uncover new facets of your family's history.

Source(s)

1. [Quick Tips for Breaking Through Your Genealogy Brick Walls | Ancestry](#)
2. [Breaking Through Your Genealogy Brick Walls | Ancestry](#)
3. [Use Land Records to Bust Genealogy Brick Walls](#)
4. [10 True Genealogy Brick Walls and How to (Possibly!) Break Through Them](#)
5. [29 Tried-and-True Brick Wall Strategies from Our Readers](#)
6. [Tips for Breaking Down Brick Walls in Genealogy](#)
7. [Genealogical Brick Walls: What They Are and How to Get Around Them](#)
8. [Overcoming Genealogical Brick Walls: Strategies and Tips](#)
9. https://youtu.be/TfbvMyD4Ibs
10. Microsoft Co-Pilot

Handling Conflicting Information

Handling conflicting information from different data sources is a common challenge in genealogy research. Here are some steps to help you resolve and document discrepancies:

1. Evaluate the Data:

- Determine whether the sources are first-hand (primary) or hear-say (secondary). Primary sources, created at the time of an event, are generally more reliable. The information shared by my grandmother are primary sources for my research. When my grandmother was uncertain, she would tell me to verify the information.

2. Cross-Check Information:

- Look for additional records that can confirm or refute the conflicting details. Refer to home documents or local sources when available.

3. Consider the Source:

- Understand the historical and cultural context that might explain why the information differs. For example, census data covered a long period of time which may cause individuals to be listed in multiple households.

4. Analyze the Evidence:

- Weigh the evidence based on its quality and relevance to your research question. Learn to discern facts from gossip. ***Lesson #2: Family history is not "gossip".***

5. Document Everything:

- Keep a detailed record of all the sources and their conflicting information for future reference. Keeping good records can eliminate headaches and retracing facts that you have already resolved.

Conflicting information is not uncommon, and sometimes it may not be possible to determine which source is correct. The key is to use critical thinking and thorough research to make the best judgment possible.

Source(s)

1. Resolving Conflicting Information in Sources - Legacy Tree
2. Conflicting Evidence in Genealogy: Examples and Solutions
3. What to Do if You Discover Conflicting Genealogy Information
4. Resolving Three Common Conflicting Evidence in Genealogy
5. Microsoft Co-pilot

Avoiding Potential Pitfalls

Genealogy research can be a rewarding endeavor, but it's also fraught with potential pitfalls that can lead you astray. Here are some common mistakes to watch out for:

1. Inaccurate Data:

- **Ages that Don't Make Sense:** Ensure the dates make sense, like children not born before their parents or women giving birth at improbable ages. However, it is not uncommon that women gave birth at younger ages and continued through older ages compared to what we traditionally see now.

2. Copying Data:

- **Data from Other Family Trees:** Always verify information from other trees before adding it to your own tree to avoid perpetuating errors. This is extremely common as many people are just copying what they see without properly researching.

3. Census Index Errors:

- **Incorrect Record Indexes:** Digitized records are not 100% accurate. Always cross-reference with the primary documents when possible.

4. Avoid Tunnel Vision:

- **Overlooking the "Entire" Family:** Focusing solely on direct ancestors can cause you to miss valuable information from siblings and other relatives. *Lesson #5 – You don't Know, what you don't know.*

5. Stay Organized:

- **Lack of Systematic Research:** Keep a well-organized research log and back up your master data to avoid losing valuable information. I can't over-stress the importance of this step. There was such a willingness to share information with me that I would write on sticky notes, napkins, or whatever writing source that I could find. My only saving grace was that I had software and would enter the information promptly!

6. Just the Facts:

- **Jumping to Conclusions:** Avoid making assumptions about relationships without solid evidence to back them up. *Lesson #4 – Don't assume anything. When in doubt, ask. Don't make an ass of yourself by guessing.*

By being aware of these pitfalls and approaching your research methodically, you can minimize errors and build a more accurate family tree. Genealogy is a meticulous process that often requires double-checking and validation of facts to ensure the integrity of your findings.

Source(s)

1. 5 Common Genealogy Errors (and How to Avoid Them) - Family Tree Magazine
2. Research Pitfalls of Beginning Genealogists - Legacy Tree
3. The 12 Important Genealogy Dos and Don'ts You Need to Know
4. Genealogy Research: 5 Common Mistakes to Avoid - Geni.com
5. 6 Common Genealogy Mistakes And How To Avoid Them
6. Microsoft Co-Pilot

Enjoy the Journey!

Understanding your roots and heritage is an asset to many families. My research documents our history in American back to 1865. Prior to 1865 some dates may be hard to document or verify 100%. But our family history will not be lost due to threats of banning books or taking an extreme poetic license to rewriting history.

The fact that you exist today and are searching to learn more about your ancestors means that their legacy and history has not been lost. Knowing who you are and the trials you've come through makes you a conqueror of your own destiny.

When I begin this genealogy journey, I did not understand why. But now I understand, without question, that I have been a good caretaker of our family history. I have not been selfish or ashamed of my history. I am empowered to live and speak with authority.

Knowing who I am does not make me "too black" or a feminist. Neither of which I am ashamed of! Requiring that you speak to me with respect does not make me militant or an angry woman. Requiring that you speak my name correctly is to acknowledge that I exist. Respect not afforded to our ancestors.

This journey does not end with me. That which I have learned, I eagerly pass on to the next generation so they may become good caretakers of our history. It is what my grandmother wanted. I have been determined and undeterred to keep her spirit and legacy alive.

When you reflect, remember the history of the strong women and men who came before us. Many sacrificed their bodies, and their children yet they never surrendered to their circumstances. Our ancestors simply whispered the words of hope to their children, so they understood that they are never alone and that they have family. Seeing images of strong men and women empowers my soul to understand that there are no obstacles or circumstances that can't be overcome.

I have corresponded with family across this country. People whom I never met but feel connected as they share the same spoken stories and possibly the same DNA. It is that connecting of the hearts that makes us family.

As I confidently prepare to pass my family history to the next generation, know that I am equally confident that you will be good caretakers of your family history.

Lesson: #8

Be proud of who you are.

Jeannette Golden

Tribute to Our Queens

**Dedicated to
Mom and Grandma
who changed by life.**

In every line of her storied face,
A tale of triumph, not of disgrace.
Through trials and time, she stands tall,
A mighty force, she won't let fall.

Her hands, they've worked the hardest fields,
Yet, in her grasp, the future yields.
She sews the seeds of hope and fight,
In darkest hours, she is the light.

From whispered prayers in the night's embrace,
To loud protests in the market's space.
She's the guardian of her kin's dreams,
The matriarch, the queen of schemes.

Her laughter, a melody of strength,
It carries far, it goes great lengths.
To soothe the pain, to heal the rift,
Her very presence is a gift.

Generations of wisdom in her eyes,
She sees through falsehoods and the lies.
With every challenge, she's grown keener,
A resilient spirit, rarely seen.

She's not just another in the crowd,
Her voice is clear, her spirit loud.
She's the protector of her family's flame,
In her, there's power, there's no shame.

So, let's honor her, let's sing her praise,
For African American women, the torch ablaze.
For they are the pillars on which we lean,
In them, the greatest strength is seen.

May this poem serve as a tribute to the enduring spirit and
unwavering strength of African American women across
generations.

Created with Microsoft Co-Pilot

Tribute to Our Warrior Kings

**For my
Brother and Kings
who protected me my entire life.**

In every heart, there lies a beat,
A rhythm strong, a defiant feat,
Of African American men who rise,
Against the tide of stereotypes and lies.

They stand tall, amidst the storm,
With courage fierce, they break the norm,
Protectors of their kin so dear,
Their love resounding, crystal clear.

Through history's pages, they've carved a path,
With every step, they've faced the wrath,
Yet, undeterred, they've held their ground,
In their resolve, they are profound.

They've climbed the mountains, crossed the seas,
In their spirit, there's an endless breeze,
Of hope and dreams, they've paved the way,
For brighter nights and richer days.

Role models, mentors, leaders true,
Their legacy is a vibrant hue,
Of perseverance, grace, and might,
Guiding the young from darkness to light.

So, here's to the men who've overcome,
Whose battles fought, have victories won,
May their stories echo, inspire,
And light up the world with their undying fire.

This poem is a tribute to the enduring spirit and positive impact of African American men who have overcome adversity and continue to inspire future generations.

Created with Microsoft Co-Pilot